TABLE OF CONTENTS

1. Introduction to Java Programming
2. Understanding BlueJ: Your First Java Environment
3. Basics of Java: Variables, Data Types, and Operators
4. Control Structures: If Statements and Loops
5. Object-Oriented Programming: Classes and Objects
6. Methods and Parameters: Building Blocks of Java
7. Arrays and ArrayLists: Managing Data Collections
8. Inheritance and Polymorphism: Advanced OOP Concepts
9. Exception Handling: Writing Robust Code
10. File Handling in Java: Reading and Writing Files
11. GUI Programming: Creating Windows with Swing
12. Applets and JavaFX: Advanced GUI Techniques
13. Java Libraries: Utilizing Built-in Functions
14. Debugging and Testing: Ensuring Code

Quality

15. Project: Creating a Comprehensive Java Application

INTRODUCTION

Java Programming for ICSE Students is a comprehensive guide tailored to meet the needs of high school students preparing for their ICSE examinations. Java, known for its simplicity and readability, is an ideal language for beginners and this book aims to make learning Java an enjoyable and enriching experience. The book is structured to provide a step-by-step approach to learning Java, starting from the basics and gradually moving to more complex concepts. By the end of this book, students will have a solid foundation in Java programming and be well-prepared for their exams and future programming endeavors.

Java is a versatile and powerful programming language used widely in various applications, from web development to mobile applications and enterprise solutions. Its platform-independent nature, supported by the Java Virtual Machine (JVM), makes it a popular choice among developers. For ICSE students, mastering Java not only helps in scoring well in exams but also opens up numerous opportunities in the field of software development.

This book begins with an introduction to Java programming, explaining the significance of Java and its evolution over the years. It then delves into BlueJ, an integrated development environment (IDE) specifically designed for educational purposes. BlueJ provides a user-friendly interface for writing, compiling, and debugging Java programs, making it an excellent tool for beginners.

The chapters are meticulously crafted to ensure a gradual learning curve. Starting with the basics of Java, including variables, data types, and operators, students will learn to write simple programs. As they progress, they will explore control structures, such as if statements and loops, which are essential for making decisions and repeating tasks in programs.

Object-oriented programming (OOP) is a core concept in Java, and this book provides an in-depth understanding of classes and objects, which are the building blocks of OOP. Students will learn how to define classes, create objects, and utilize methods and parameters to enhance the functionality of their programs.

Managing data collections efficiently is crucial, and this book covers arrays and ArrayLists, enabling students to store and manipulate large sets of data. Advanced OOP concepts, such as inheritance and polymorphism, are also explained in detail, allowing students to create more sophisticated programs.

Writing robust code is an essential skill for any programmer. This book introduces exception handling, teaching students how to handle errors gracefully and ensure the reliability of their programs. Additionally, file handling in Java is covered, enabling students to read from and write to files, a common requirement in many applications.

Graphical user interface (GUI) programming is another exciting aspect of Java. Students will learn to create windows and interactive elements using Swing and explore advanced GUI techniques with Applets and JavaFX. Utilizing built-in Java libraries can significantly simplify programming tasks, and this book demonstrates how to make the most of these powerful tools.

Ensuring code quality is vital, and this book emphasizes the importance of debugging and testing. Students will learn various techniques to identify and fix errors in their code, as well as write test cases to validate their programs.

The book culminates in a comprehensive project, where students apply the concepts they have learned to create a complete Java application. This hands-on experience reinforces their understanding and prepares them for real-world programming challenges.

Java Programming for ICSE Students is more than just a textbook; it is a complete learning resource designed to inspire and empower students. With clear explanations, practical examples, and numerous exercises, this book makes learning Java an engaging and rewarding journey. Whether you are a novice or have some programming experience, this book will guide you through the fascinating world of Java programming and help you achieve your academic and professional goals.

CHAPTER 1: INTRODUCTION TO JAVA PROGRAMMING

Java is a high-level, object-oriented programming language developed by Sun Microsystems in the mid-1990s. It was designed to be platform-independent, which means that Java programs can run on any device equipped with the Java Virtual Machine (JVM). This "write once, run anywhere" capability has contributed to Java's widespread adoption in various fields, from web development to mobile applications and enterprise software.

The history of Java dates back to the early 1990s when James Gosling, Mike Sheridan, and Patrick Naughton started the Green Project at Sun Microsystems. The project aimed to create a language for programming home appliances, but it soon evolved into something much more significant. The first public implementation of Java, Java 1.0, was released in 1995, and it quickly gained popularity due to its robustness, security features, and cross-platform capabilities.

Java's syntax is heavily influenced by C and C++, but it simplifies many complex aspects of these languages, making it more accessible to beginners.

One of Java's key features is its automatic memory management, which eliminates the need for manual memory allocation and deallocation, reducing the risk of memory leaks and other related issues.

In addition to its platform independence, Java is known for its security features. The language was designed with a strong emphasis on security, making it a preferred choice for developing applications that handle sensitive data. Java's built-in security features include bytecode verification, which ensures that code adheres to certain security constraints, and the Java security manager, which allows developers to set policies for what code can and cannot do.

Java is also renowned for its performance. While it may not match the speed of languages like C or C++, its performance is more than adequate for most applications. The Just-In-Time (JIT) compiler, introduced in Java 1.2, significantly improves the performance of Java applications by compiling bytecode into native machine code at runtime.

Another strength of Java is its extensive standard library, which provides a wide range of pre-built classes and methods for various programming tasks. This library includes classes for data structures, mathematical operations, file handling, networking, and much more. By leveraging these built-in functions, developers can write efficient and effective code without reinventing the wheel.

In the context of ICSE (Indian Certificate of Secondary Education) curriculum, learning Java provides students with a strong foundation in programming.

The ICSE syllabus emphasizes problem-solving skills, logical thinking, and the application of programming concepts to real-world scenarios. By mastering Java, students can develop these essential skills and prepare themselves for advanced studies and careers in computer science and related fields.

The first chapter of this book will cover the following topics:

- Introduction to Java and its features
- Setting up the Java development environment
- Writing and running your first Java program
- Understanding the basic structure of a Java program
- Overview of Java syntax and conventions

By the end of this chapter, students will have a clear understanding of what Java is, how it works, and how to set up their development environment to start writing Java programs. They will also write their first Java program, which will serve as a foundation for the more complex programs they will create in subsequent chapters.

Setting Up the Java Development Environment

Before diving into Java programming, it's essential to set up your development environment. For ICSE students, we recommend using BlueJ, an integrated development environment (IDE) designed specifically for educational purposes. BlueJ provides a simple and intuitive interface, making it easy for beginners to write, compile, and debug Java programs.

To set up BlueJ, follow these steps:

1. **Download and Install BlueJ**: Visit the official BlueJ website (https://bluej.org) and download the latest version of the software for your operating system. Follow the installation instructions to complete the setup.
2. **Install the Java Development Kit (JDK)**: BlueJ requires the JDK to compile and run Java programs. The JDK can be downloaded from the Oracle website (https://www.oracle.com/java/technologies/javase-downloads.html). Make sure to download the version compatible with your operating system and follow the installation instructions.
3. **Configure BlueJ**: Once BlueJ and the JDK are installed, launch BlueJ. You may need to configure the IDE to use the correct JDK path. This can typically be done in the BlueJ preferences or settings menu.
4. **Create a New Project**: In BlueJ, create a new project by selecting Project -> New Project from the menu. Choose a suitable name and location for your project.
5. **Write Your First Program**: Inside your new project, create a new class by selecting Class -> New Class. Name the class HelloWorld and ensure it is set to create a Class template. Double-click the new class to open the code editor and replace the template code with the following:

java

```
public class HelloWorld {
    public static void main(String[] args) {
        System.out.println("Hello, World!");
    }
}
```

6. **Compile and Run the Program**: Click the compile button to compile your code. If there are no errors, right-click the HelloWorld class and select void main(String[] args) to run your program. You should see the output Hello, World! in the BlueJ terminal window.

Congratulations! You have successfully written and run your first Java program. This simple program demonstrates the basic structure of a Java application and serves as a starting point for your journey into Java programming.

CHAPTER 2: UNDERSTANDING BLUEJ: YOUR FIRST JAVA ENVIRONMENT

BlueJ is an integrated development environment (IDE) specifically designed for teaching and learning Java programming. It provides a user-friendly interface that simplifies the process of writing, compiling, and debugging Java programs. In this chapter, we will explore the features of BlueJ and learn how to navigate the IDE effectively.

Overview of BlueJ Interface

The BlueJ interface consists of several key components:

1. **Project Window**: The main window where you can create and manage your projects. It displays a graphical representation of the classes in your project and their relationships.
2. **Class Diagram**: A visual representation of the classes in your project. It helps you understand the structure of your program and the relationships between different classes.

3. **Code Editor**: The editor where you write your Java code. It provides syntax highlighting, auto-indentation, and other features to make coding easier.
4. **Terminal Window**: A window where the output of your programs is displayed. It also allows you to interact with your programs by entering input if required.
5. **Object Bench**: A space where you can create and manipulate objects of your classes. It allows you to test your classes and methods interactively.

Creating and Managing Projects

In BlueJ, a project is a container for your Java classes and resources. To create a new project, select Project -> New Project from the menu. Choose a suitable name and location for your project. Once the project is created, you can add classes and start writing your code.

Writing and Running Java Programs

To write a Java program in BlueJ, follow these steps:

1. **Create a New Class**: In the project window, select Class -> New Class. Name the class and choose a suitable template (e.g., Class for a standard class).
2. **Write Your Code**: Double-click the new class to open the code editor. Replace the template code with your Java code.
3. **Compile the Code**: Click the compile button (represented by a checkmark) to compile your code. BlueJ will highlight any errors in your

code and provide suggestions for fixing them.
   4. **Run the Program**: Right-click the class in the project window and select void main(String[] args) to run the program. The output will be displayed in the terminal window.

Debugging and Testing

BlueJ provides several tools to help you debug and test your programs:
   1. **Breakpoints**: You can set breakpoints in your code to pause execution at specific lines. This allows you to inspect the state of your program and identify any issues.
   2. **Step Through Code**: Once a breakpoint is reached, you can step through your code line by line to see how it executes.
   3. **Inspect Variables**: BlueJ allows you to inspect the values of variables at any point in your program. This is useful for understanding how your program manipulates data.
   4. **Object Bench**: The object bench allows you to create and interact with objects of your classes. You can call methods on these objects and see the results immediately.

Example: Creating a Simple Calculator

Let's create a simple calculator program in BlueJ to demonstrate these concepts. Follow these steps:
   1. **Create a New Project**: Select Project -> New Project and name it Calculator.
   2. **Create a New Class**: In the project window, select Class -> New Class and name it Calculator.

3. **Write the Code**: Double-click the Calculator class to open the code editor. Replace the template code with the following:

```java
public class Calculator {
    public int add(int a, int b) {
        return a + b;
    }

    public int subtract(int a, int b) {
        return a - b;
    }

    public int multiply(int a, int b) {
        return a * b;
    }

    public int divide(int a, int b) {
        if (b == 0) {
            throw new IllegalArgumentException("Division by zero is not allowed.");
        }
        return a / b;
    }

    public static void main(String[] args) {
        Calculator calc = new Calculator();
        System.out.println("Addition: " + calc.add(5, 3));
        System.out.println("Subtraction: " + calc.subtract(5, 3));
        System.out.println("Multiplication: " + calc.multiply(5, 3));
        System.out.println("Division: " + calc.divide(5, 3));
    }
}
```

4. **Compile the Code**: Click the compile button to

compile your code.

5. **Run the Program**: Right-click the Calculator class and select void main(String[] args) to run the program. The output will be displayed in the terminal window.

6. **Test the Methods**: Use the object bench to create an instance of the Calculator class and call its methods interactively. Right-click the Calculator class, select new Calculator(), and then call methods like add, subtract, multiply, and divide.

By the end of this chapter, students will be comfortable using BlueJ to create, manage, and test Java programs. They will understand the basic features of the IDE and be able to write simple Java programs with confidence.

CHAPTER 3: BASICS OF JAVA: VARIABLES, DATA TYPES, AND OPERATORS

In this chapter, we will explore the fundamental building blocks of Java programming: variables, data types, and operators. These concepts form the foundation of any Java program and are essential for writing effective and efficient code.

Variables

Variables are used to store data that can be manipulated by a program. In Java, a variable must be declared before it can be used. The syntax for declaring a variable is as follows:

java

```
dataType variableName;
```

For example:

java

```
int age;
double salary;
String name;
```

After declaring a variable, you can assign a value to it

using the assignment operator (=):

java

```
age = 25;
salary = 50000.0;
name = "John Doe";
```

You can also declare and initialize a variable in a single statement:

java

```
int age = 25;
double salary = 50000.0;
String name = "John Doe";
```

Data Types

Java is a strongly-typed language, which means that every variable must have a data type. Data types define the kind of data that can be stored in a variable. Java has two categories of data types: primitive data types and reference data types.

1. **Primitive Data Types**: These are the most basic data types and include:
   - byte: **8-bit integer**
   - short: **16-bit integer**
   - int: **32-bit integer**
   - long: **64-bit integer**
   - float: **32-bit floating-point number**
   - double: **64-bit floating-point number**
   - char: **16-bit Unicode character**
   - boolean: **true or false**

For example:

java

```java
int age = 25;
double salary = 50000.0;
char grade = 'A';
boolean isStudent = true;
```

2. **Reference Data Types**: These include objects and arrays. Reference data types store references to objects rather than the objects themselves. The most commonly used reference data type is String.

For example:

java

```java
String name = "John Doe";
int[] numbers = {1, 2, 3, 4, 5};
```

Operators

Operators are used to perform operations on variables and values. Java provides several types of operators:

1. **Arithmetic Operators**: These operators perform basic arithmetic operations:
    - + (addition)
    - - (subtraction)
    - * (multiplication)
    - / (division)
    - % (modulus)

For example:

java

```java
int a = 10;
int b = 5;
int sum = a + b; // 15
int difference = a - b; // 5
```

```java
int product = a * b; // 50
int quotient = a / b; // 2
int remainder = a % b; // 0
```

2. **Relational Operators**: These operators compare two values and return a boolean result:
    - == (equal to)
    - != (not equal to)
    - > (greater than)
    - < (less than)
    - >= (greater than or equal to)
    - <= (less than or equal to)

For example:

java

```java
int a = 10;
int b = 5;
boolean isEqual = (a == b); // false
boolean isNotEqual = (a != b); // true
boolean isGreater = (a > b); // true
boolean isLesser = (a < b); // false
```

3. **Logical Operators**: These operators are used to combine multiple boolean expressions:
    - && (logical AND)
    - || (logical OR)
    - ! (logical NOT)

For example:

java

```java
boolean a = true;
boolean b = false;
boolean result = (a && b); // false
```

```
boolean resultOr = (a || b); // true
boolean resultNot = !a; // false
```

4. **Assignment Operators**: These operators are used to assign values to variables:
    - = (assignment)
    - += (addition assignment)
    - -= (subtraction assignment)
    - *= (multiplication assignment)
    - /= (division assignment)
    - %= (modulus assignment)

For example:

java

```
int a = 10;
a += 5; // a = a + 5; a = 15
a -= 3; // a = a - 3; a = 12
a *= 2; // a = a * 2; a = 24
a /= 4; // a = a / 4; a = 6
a %= 2; // a = a % 2; a = 0
```

5. **Increment and Decrement Operators**: These operators are used to increase or decrease the value of a variable by 1:
    - ++ (increment)
    - -- (decrement)

For example:

java

```
int a = 10;
a++; // a = a + 1; a = 11
a--; // a = a - 1; a = 10
```

By understanding and mastering variables, data types, and operators, students will be able to write more complex and powerful Java programs. These fundamental concepts are essential for any programmer and will serve as the building blocks for more advanced topics covered in the subsequent chapters.

CHAPTER 4: CONTROL STRUCTURES: IF STATEMENTS AND LOOPS

Control structures are essential components of any programming language, allowing the flow of execution to be directed based on certain conditions. Java provides several control structures to help you manage the flow of your programs: if statements and loops are among the most commonly used.

If Statements

If statements are used to execute a block of code only if a specified condition is true. The syntax for an if statement is:

java

```
if (condition) {
    // code to be executed if the condition is true
}
```

For example:

java

```
int age = 18;
if (age >= 18) {
```

```
    System.out.println("You are an adult.");
}
```

If-Else Statements

Sometimes you want to execute one block of code if a condition is true and another block if it is false. This can be done using an if-else statement:

java

```java
if (condition) {
    // code to be executed if the condition is true
} else {
    // code to be executed if the condition is false
}
```

For example:

java

```java
int age = 16;
if (age >= 18) {
    System.out.println("You are an adult.");
} else {
    System.out.println("You are a minor.");
}
```

Else-If Ladder

If you have multiple conditions to check, you can use an else-if ladder:

java

```java
if (condition1) {
    // code to be executed if condition1 is true
} else if (condition2) {
    // code to be executed if condition2 is true
} else {
    // code to be executed if both conditions are false
}
```

For example:

```java
int marks = 85;
if (marks >= 90) {
    System.out.println("Grade: A+");
} else if (marks >= 80) {
    System.out.println("Grade: A");
} else if (marks >= 70) {
    System.out.println("Grade: B");
} else {
    System.out.println("Grade: C");
}
```

Loops

Loops allow you to execute a block of code repeatedly based on a condition. Java provides several types of loops: for loops, while loops, and do-while loops.

For Loop

A for loop is used to repeat a block of code a specific number of times. The syntax for a for loop is:

```java
for (initialization; condition; increment/decrement) {
    // code to be executed
}
```

For example:

```java
for (int i = 0; i < 5; i++) {
    System.out.println("Value of i: " + i);
}
```

While Loop

A while loop repeats a block of code as long as a specified condition is true. The syntax for a while loop is:

```java
while (condition) {
    // code to be executed
}
```

For example:

```java
int i = 0;
while (i < 5) {
    System.out.println("Value of i: " + i);
    i++;
}
```

Do-While Loop

A do-while loop is similar to a while loop, but it guarantees that the block of code will be executed at least once. The syntax for a do-while loop is:

```java
do {
    // code to be executed
} while (condition);
```

For example:

```java
int i = 0;
do {
    System.out.println("Value of i: " + i);
    i++;
} while (i < 5);
```

Nested Loops

Loops can be nested within other loops. This is useful for working with multi-dimensional arrays or performing repeated operations within repeated operations.

For example:

java

```
for (int i = 0; i < 3; i++) {
   for (int j = 0; j < 3; j++) {
      System.out.println("i: " + i + ", j: " + j);
   }
}
```

Example: Simple Calculator Using If Statements and Loops

Let's create a simple calculator that performs basic arithmetic operations (addition, subtraction, multiplication, division) based on user input. The program will use if statements to determine the operation and a while loop to allow multiple calculations until the user decides to exit.

java

```
import java.util.Scanner;

public class SimpleCalculator {
   public static void main(String[] args) {
      Scanner scanner = new Scanner(System.in);
      boolean continueCalculating = true;

      while (continueCalculating) {
         System.out.println("Enter first number:");
         double num1 = scanner.nextDouble();

         System.out.println("Enter an operator (+, -, *, /):");
         char operator = scanner.next().charAt(0);

         System.out.println("Enter second number:");
         double num2 = scanner.nextDouble();

         double result;
```

```java
        switch (operator) {
            case '+':
                result = num1 + num2;
                break;
            case '-':
                result = num1 - num2;
                break;
            case '*':
                result = num1 + num2;
                break;
            case '/':
                if (num2 != 0) {
                    result = num1 / num2;
                } else {
                    System.out.println("Error: Division by zero is not allowed.");
                    continue;
                }
                break;
            default:
                System.out.println("Invalid operator.");
                continue;
        }

        System.out.println("Result: " + result);
        System.out.println("Do you want to perform another calculation? (yes/no)");
        String userResponse = scanner.next();

        if (!userResponse.equalsIgnoreCase("yes")) {
            continueCalculating = false;
        }
    }

    scanner.close();
    System.out.println("Calculator has exited.");
```

    }
}

This program demonstrates the use of if statements, a switch-case statement, and a while loop to create a simple calculator. By following these examples and practicing with different scenarios, students will gain a solid understanding of control structures in Java.

CHAPTER 5: OBJECT-ORIENTED PROGRAMMING: CLASSES AND OBJECTS

Object-oriented programming (OOP) is a fundamental concept in Java, where programs are organized around objects rather than actions. Understanding classes and objects is crucial for writing effective Java programs. This chapter will introduce the key concepts of OOP and demonstrate how to create and use classes and objects.

Classes and Objects

A class is a blueprint for creating objects, defining the properties (fields) and behaviors (methods) that the objects will have. An object is an instance of a class, created using the new keyword.

Defining a Class

To define a class in Java, use the class keyword followed by the class name and a pair of curly braces to enclose the class body:

java

```java
public class Person {
    // fields (properties)
    String name;
    int age;

    // methods (behaviors)
    void introduce() {
        System.out.println("Hello, my name is " + name + " and I am " + age + " years old.");
    }
}
```

Creating Objects

To create an object of a class, use the `new` keyword followed by the class constructor:

java

```java
public class Main {
    public static void main(String[] args) {
        // creating an object of the Person class
        Person person1 = new Person();
        person1.name = "John";
        person1.age = 30;
        person1.introduce();
    }
}
```

This program creates an object `person1` of the `Person` class, assigns values to its fields, and calls its `introduce` method.

Constructors

Constructors are special methods used to initialize objects. They have the same name as the class and do not have a return type. A constructor is called when an object is created.

java

```java
public class Person {
    String name;
    int age;

    // constructor
    public Person(String name, int age) {
        this.name = name;
        this.age = age;
    }

    void introduce() {
        System.out.println("Hello, my name is " + name + " and I am " + age + " years old.");
    }
}
```

To create an object using the constructor:

java

```java
public class Main {
    public static void main(String[] args) {
        Person person1 = new Person("John", 30);
        person1.introduce();
    }
}
```

Encapsulation

Encapsulation is the practice of keeping fields (variables) private and providing public methods to access and modify them. This helps to protect the data and ensure it is used correctly.

java

```java
public class Person {
    private String name;
    private int age;
```

```java
    // constructor
    public Person(String name, int age) {
        this.name = name;
        this.age = age;
    }

    // getter method for name
    public String getName() {
        return name;
    }

    // setter method for name
    public void setName(String name) {
        this.name = name;
    }

    // getter method for age
    public int getAge() {
        return age;
    }

    // setter method for age
    public void setAge(int age) {
        this.age = age;
    }

    void introduce() {
        System.out.println("Hello, my name is " + name + " and I am " + age + " years old.");
    }
}
```

This approach ensures that the `name` and `age` fields can only be accessed and modified through the `getName`, `setName`, `getAge`, and `setAge` methods, providing better control over the data.

Inheritance

Inheritance is a mechanism that allows one class (subclass) to inherit the properties and methods of another class (superclass). This promotes code reuse and establishes a hierarchical relationship between classes.

java

```java
public class Animal {
   void makeSound() {
      System.out.println("Some sound...");
   }
}

public class Dog extends Animal {
   void bark() {
      System.out.println("Woof!");
   }
}

public class Main {
   public static void main(String[] args) {
      Dog dog = new Dog();
      dog.makeSound(); // inherited method
      dog.bark(); // subclass method
   }
}
```

Polymorphism

Polymorphism allows objects of different classes to be treated as objects of a common superclass. It is achieved through method overriding and interface implementation.

java

```java
public class Animal {
   void makeSound() {
```

```java
        System.out.println("Some sound...");
    }
}
public class Dog extends Animal {
    @Override
    void makeSound() {
        System.out.println("Woof!");
    }
}
public class Cat extends Animal {
    @Override
    void makeSound() {
        System.out.println("Meow!");
    }
}
public class Main {
    public static void main(String[] args) {
        Animal myDog = new Dog();
        Animal myCat = new Cat();
        myDog.makeSound(); // Woof!
        myCat.makeSound(); // Meow!
    }
}
```

In this example, the `makeSound` method is overridden in both the `Dog` and `Cat` classes, allowing different behaviors based on the object's actual type.

By mastering classes, objects, inheritance, and polymorphism, students will be able to create complex and well-structured Java programs. These object-oriented programming principles are fundamental to understanding and applying Java effectively.

CHAPTER 6: METHODS AND PARAMETERS: BUILDING BLOCKS OF JAVA

Methods are the building blocks of Java programs. They allow you to encapsulate code into reusable units, making your programs more modular and easier to maintain. This chapter will cover the basics of defining, calling, and using methods, as well as passing parameters and returning values.

Defining Methods

A method is defined with a return type, a name, a pair of parentheses (which may contain parameters), and a body enclosed in curly braces:

java

```
returnType    methodName(parameter1Type    parameter1, parameter2Type parameter2, ...) {
    // method body
}
```

For example:

java

```
public class Calculator {
```

```java
    // method to add two numbers
    public int add(int a, int b) {
        return a + b;
    }

    // method to subtract two numbers
    public int subtract(int a, int b) {
        return a - b;
    }
}
```

Calling Methods

To call a method, use the method name followed by a pair of parentheses, passing any required arguments:

java

```java
public class Main {
    public static void main(String[] args) {
        Calculator calc = new Calculator();
        int sum = calc.add(5, 3);
        int difference = calc.subtract(5, 3);
        System.out.println("Sum: " + sum);
        System.out.println("Difference: " + difference);
    }
}
```

Passing Parameters

Parameters allow you to pass data into methods. Parameters are specified within the parentheses of the method definition:

java

```java
public class Printer {
    // method with a single parameter
    public void printMessage(String message) {
        System.out.println(message);
    }
```

```java
}
public class Main {
    public static void main(String[] args) {
        Printer printer = new Printer();
        printer.printMessage("Hello, World!");
    }
}
```

Returning Values

Methods can return values using the `return` keyword. The return type of the method must match the type of value being returned:

java

```java
public class Calculator {
    // method to multiply two numbers
    public int multiply(int a, int b) {
        return a * b;
    }

    // method to divide two numbers
    public double divide(int a, int b) {
        if (b == 0) {
            throw new IllegalArgumentException("Division by zero is not allowed.");
        }
        return (double) a / b;
    }
}
public class Main {
    public static void main(String[] args) {
        Calculator calc = new Calculator();
        int product = calc.multiply(5, 3);
        double quotient = calc.divide(5, 3);
        System.out.println("Product: " + product);
```

```
        System.out.println("Quotient: " + quotient);
    }
}
```

Method Overloading

Method overloading allows you to define multiple methods with the same name but different parameters. This enables you to provide different implementations based on the number or type of arguments passed.

java

```java
public class Calculator {
    // method to add two integers
    public int add(int a, int b) {
        return a + b;
    }

    // method to add three integers
    public int add(int a, int b, int c) {
        return a + b + c;
    }

    // method to add two doubles
    public double add(double a, double b) {
        return a + b;
    }
}
public class Main {
    public static void main(String[] args) {
        Calculator calc = new Calculator();
        int sum1 = calc.add(5, 3);
        int sum2 = calc.add(5, 3, 2);
        double sum3 = calc.add(5.0, 3.0);
        System.out.println("Sum1: " + sum1);
        System.out.println("Sum2: " + sum2);
        System.out.println("Sum3: " + sum3);
```

    }
}

Example: Banking Application

Let's create a simple banking application that uses methods to perform various operations such as deposit, withdrawal, and checking the balance.

java

```java
public class BankAccount {
    private String accountNumber;
    private double balance;

    public BankAccount(String accountNumber, double initialBalance) {
        this.accountNumber = accountNumber;
        this.balance = initialBalance;
    }

    // method to deposit money
    public void deposit(double amount) {
        if (amount > 0) {
            balance += amount;
            System.out.println("Deposited: " + amount);
        } else {
            System.out.println("Invalid deposit amount.");
        }
    }

    // method to withdraw money
    public void withdraw(double amount) {
        if (amount > 0 && amount <= balance) {
            balance -= amount;
            System.out.println("Withdrew: " + amount);
        } else {
            System.out.println("Invalid withdrawal amount.");
        }
```

```java
    }

    // method to check the balance
    public double getBalance() {
        return balance;
    }

    public static void main(String[] args) {
        BankAccount account = new BankAccount("123456", 1000.0);
        account.deposit(500.0);
        account.withdraw(200.0);
        System.out.println("Current Balance: " + account.getBalance());
    }
}
```

In this example, the BankAccount class has methods for depositing, withdrawing, and checking the balance. The main method demonstrates how to create a bank account object and perform various operations.

By understanding and practicing with methods and parameters, students will be able to create more modular and reusable code. These concepts are essential for building complex applications and improving code maintainability.

CHAPTER 7: ARRAYS AND ARRAYLISTS: MANAGING DATA COLLECTIONS

Arrays and ArrayLists are essential data structures in Java, used to store and manipulate collections of data. This chapter will cover the basics of arrays, ArrayLists, and the differences between them, providing practical examples to help you understand their usage.

Arrays

An array is a fixed-size, ordered collection of elements of the same type. The size of an array is determined when it is created and cannot be changed.

Declaring and Initializing Arrays

To declare and initialize an array, use the following syntax:

java

```
// declaration
dataType[] arrayName;
```

```
// initialization
arrayName = new dataType[size];
```

// declaration and initialization in one step

```
dataType[] arrayName = new dataType[size];
```

// initialization with values
```
dataType[] arrayName = {value1, value2, value3, ...};
```

For example:

java

```
int[] numbers = new int[5];
numbers[0] = 10;
numbers[1] = 20;
numbers[2] = 30;
numbers[3] = 40;
numbers[4] = 50;

// or

int[] numbers = {10, 20, 30, 40, 50};
```

Accessing and Modifying Array Elements

Array elements are accessed and modified using their index, which starts from 0:

java

```
int firstNumber = numbers[0]; // 10
numbers[1] = 25; // changing the value at index 1
```

Looping Through Arrays

You can use loops to iterate through array elements:

java

```
for (int i = 0; i < numbers.length; i++) {
    System.out.println("Element at index " + i + ": " + numbers[i]);
}
```

You can also use enhanced for loop:

java

```
for (int number : numbers) {
    System.out.println(number);
}
```

ArrayLists

An ArrayList is a resizable array implementation provided by the java.util package. Unlike arrays, ArrayLists can grow and shrink in size dynamically.

Importing ArrayList

To use an ArrayList, you need to import the java.util.ArrayList class:

```java
import java.util.ArrayList;
```

Declaring and Initializing ArrayLists

To declare and initialize an ArrayList, use the following syntax:

```java
ArrayList<dataType> arrayListName = new ArrayList<dataType>();
```

For example:

```java
import java.util.ArrayList;

ArrayList<Integer> numbers = new ArrayList<Integer>();
numbers.add(10);
numbers.add(20);
numbers.add(30);
```

Accessing and Modifying ArrayList Elements

ArrayList elements are accessed and modified using their index:

```java
int firstNumber = numbers.get(0); // 10
numbers.set(1, 25); // changing the value at index 1
```

Looping Through ArrayLists

You can use loops to iterate through ArrayList elements:

java

```
for (int i = 0; i < numbers.size(); i++) {
    System.out.println("Element at index " + i + ": " + numbers.get(i));
}
```

You can also use enhanced for loop:

java

```
for (int number : numbers) {
    System.out.println(number);
}
```

Differences Between Arrays and ArrayLists

- **Size**: Arrays have a fixed size, while ArrayLists are resizable.
- **Type**: Arrays can store primitive types and objects, while ArrayLists can only store objects.
- **Performance**: Arrays are faster for accessing and modifying elements, while ArrayLists provide more flexibility with dynamic resizing.

Example: Student Grades Management

Let's create a program to manage student grades using arrays and ArrayLists.

java

```
import java.util.ArrayList;

public class StudentGrades {
    public static void main(String[] args) {
        // using an array
        int[] gradesArray = {85, 90, 78, 92, 88};

        // using an ArrayList
```

```java
        ArrayList<Integer> gradesList = new ArrayList<Integer>();
        gradesList.add(85);
        gradesList.add(90);
        gradesList.add(78);
        gradesList.add(92);
        gradesList.add(88);

        // printing array elements
        System.out.println("Grades (Array):");
        for (int i = 0; i < gradesArray.length; i++) {
            System.out.println("Student " + (i + 1) + ": " + gradesArray[i]);
        }

        // printing ArrayList elements
        System.out.println("\nGrades (ArrayList):");
        for (int i = 0; i < gradesList.size(); i++) {
            System.out.println("Student " + (i + 1) + ": " + gradesList.get(i));
        }

        // adding a new grade to the ArrayList
        gradesList.add(95);
        System.out.println("\nNew grade added to ArrayList.");

        // printing updated ArrayList elements
        System.out.println("Updated Grades (ArrayList):");
        for (int grade : gradesList) {
            System.out.println(grade);
        }
    }
}
```

In this example, the program demonstrates how to use arrays and ArrayLists to manage student grades. The ArrayList allows for dynamic resizing, making it easy to add new grades.

By understanding and practicing with arrays and ArrayLists, students will be able to manage and manipulate collections of data efficiently. These data structures are fundamental for solving complex problems and developing robust applications.

CHAPTER 8: INHERITANCE AND POLYMORPHISM: ADVANCED OOP CONCEPTS

Inheritance and polymorphism are advanced object-oriented programming (OOP) concepts that enable code reuse and flexibility. This chapter will cover the basics of inheritance, method overriding, polymorphism, and their practical applications.

Inheritance

Inheritance is a mechanism that allows one class (subclass) to inherit the properties and methods of another class (superclass). This promotes code reuse and establishes a hierarchical relationship between classes.

Defining a Superclass

A superclass is a general class that defines common properties and methods:

java

```
public class Animal {
```

```java
    void makeSound() {
        System.out.println("Some sound...");
    }
}
```

Defining a Subclass

A subclass is a specialized class that inherits from a superclass. Use the extends keyword to define a subclass:

java

```java
public class Dog extends Animal {
    void bark() {
        System.out.println("Woof!");
    }
}
```

Creating Objects

You can create objects of both the superclass and subclass:

java

```java
public class Main {
    public static void main(String[] args) {
        Animal animal = new Animal();
        Dog dog = new Dog();
        animal.makeSound();
        dog.makeSound();
        dog.bark();
    }
}
```

Method Overriding

Method overriding allows a subclass to provide a specific implementation of a method already defined in its superclass. This is useful for achieving polymorphism.

java

```java
public class Animal {
   void makeSound() {
      System.out.println("Some sound...");
   }
}
public class Dog extends Animal {
   @Override
   void makeSound() {
      System.out.println("Woof!");
   }
}
public class Cat extends Animal {
   @Override
   void makeSound() {
      System.out.println("Meow!");
   }
}
public class Main {
   public static void main(String[] args) {
      Animal myDog = new Dog();
      Animal myCat = new Cat();
      myDog.makeSound(); // Woof!
      myCat.makeSound(); // Meow!
   }
}
```

In this example, the `makeSound` method is overridden in both the `Dog` and `Cat` classes, allowing different behaviors based on the object's actual type.

Polymorphism

Polymorphism allows objects of different classes to be treated as objects of a common superclass. This is achieved through method overriding and interface implementation.

java

```java
public class Animal {
    void makeSound() {
        System.out.println("Some sound...");
    }
}

public class Dog extends Animal {
    @Override
    void makeSound() {
        System.out.println("Woof!");
    }
}

public class Cat extends Animal {
    @Override
    void makeSound() {
        System.out.println("Meow!");
    }
}

public class Main {
    public static void main(String[] args) {
        Animal myDog = new Dog();
        Animal myCat = new Cat();
        myDog.makeSound(); // Woof!
        myCat.makeSound(); // Meow!
    }
}
```

In this example, the `makeSound` method is overridden in both the `Dog` and `Cat` classes, allowing different behaviors based on the object's actual type.

Example: Library Management System

Let's create a simple library management system

that uses inheritance and polymorphism to manage different types of library items.

java

```java
public class LibraryItem {
    private String title;
    private String author;

    public LibraryItem(String title, String author) {
        this.title = title;
        this.author = author;
    }

    public String getTitle() {
        return title;
    }

    public String getAuthor() {
        return author;
    }

    public void displayInfo() {
        System.out.println("Title: " + title);
        System.out.println("Author: " + author);
    }
}

public class Book extends LibraryItem {
    private int pages;

    public Book(String title, String author, int pages) {
        super(title, author);
        this.pages = pages;
    }

    @Override
    public void displayInfo() {
        super.displayInfo();
        System.out.println("Pages: " + pages);
```

```java
    }
}
public class DVD extends LibraryItem {
    private int duration;

    public DVD(String title, String author, int duration) {
        super(title, author);
        this.duration = duration;
    }

    @Override
    public void displayInfo() {
        super.displayInfo();
        System.out.println("Duration: " + duration + " minutes");
    }
}
public class Main {
    public static void main(String[] args) {
        LibraryItem book = new Book("The Great Gatsby", "F. Scott Fitzgerald", 180);
        LibraryItem dvd = new DVD("Inception", "Christopher Nolan", 148);

        book.displayInfo();
        System.out.println();
        dvd.displayInfo();
    }
}
```

In this example, the LibraryItem class is the superclass, while the Book and DVD classes are subclasses that inherit from LibraryItem. The displayInfo method is overridden in both subclasses to provide specific information about each type of library item.

By mastering inheritance and polymorphism, students will be able to create more flexible and reusable code. These advanced OOP concepts are essential for developing complex applications and designing robust software systems.

CHAPTER 9: EXCEPTION HANDLING: WRITING ROBUST CODE

Exception handling is a mechanism that allows you to handle runtime errors and ensure your program can gracefully recover from unexpected conditions. This chapter will cover the basics of exception handling, including try-catch blocks, throwing exceptions, and creating custom exceptions.

Understanding Exceptions

An exception is an event that disrupts the normal flow of a program. Exceptions can be caused by various factors, such as invalid input, division by zero, or file not found errors. Java provides a robust exception handling mechanism to manage these situations.

Try-Catch Blocks

A try-catch block is used to handle exceptions. The code that may throw an exception is placed inside the try block, and the code to handle the exception is placed inside the catch block:

java

```java
try {
    // code that may throw an exception
} catch (ExceptionType e) {
    // code to handle the exception
}
```

For example:

java

```java
public class Main {
    public static void main(String[] args) {
        try {
            int result = 10 / 0; // this will throw an ArithmeticException
        } catch (ArithmeticException e) {
            System.out.println("Error: Division by zero is not allowed.");
        }
    }
}
```

Multiple Catch Blocks

You can use multiple catch blocks to handle different types of exceptions:

java

```java
try {
    int[] numbers = {1, 2, 3};
    System.out.println(numbers[3]); // this will throw an ArrayIndexOutOfBoundsException
} catch (ArrayIndexOutOfBoundsException e) {
    System.out.println("Error: Array index out of bounds.");
} catch (Exception e) {
    System.out.println("Error: An unexpected error occurred.");
}
```

Finally Block

A finally block is used to execute code that must run regardless of whether an exception is thrown. It is typically used for cleanup activities, such as closing resources:

java

```
try {
    // code that may throw an exception
} catch (Exception e) {
    // code to handle the exception
} finally {
    // code that will always be executed
}
```

For example:

java

```
public class Main {
    public static void main(String[] args) {
        try {
            int result = 10 / 0; // this will throw an ArithmeticException
        } catch (ArithmeticException e) {
            System.out.println("Error: Division by zero is not allowed.");
        } finally {
            System.out.println("This will always be executed.");
        }
    }
}
```

Throwing Exceptions

You can use the throw keyword to explicitly throw an exception:

java

public class Main {

```java
    public static void main(String[] args) {
        try {
            checkAge(15);
        } catch (IllegalArgumentException e) {
            System.out.println(e.getMessage());
        }
    }

    public static void checkAge(int age) {
        if (age < 18) {
            throw new IllegalArgumentException("Age must be 18 or older.");
        }
    }
}
```

Creating Custom Exceptions

You can create your own custom exceptions by extending the Exception class:

java

```java
public class InvalidAgeException extends Exception {
    public InvalidAgeException(String message) {
        super(message);
    }
}

public class Main {
    public static void main(String[] args) {
        try {
            checkAge(15);
        } catch (InvalidAgeException e) {
            System.out.println(e.getMessage());
        }
    }

    public static void checkAge(int age) throws InvalidAgeException {
```

```java
        if (age < 18) {
            throw new InvalidAgeException("Age must be 18 or older.");
        }
    }
}
```

Example: File Handling with Exception Handling

Let's create a program that reads data from a file and handles potential exceptions, such as file not found or input-output errors.

java

```java
import java.io.File;
import java.io.FileNotFoundException;
import java.util.Scanner;

public class FileReader {
    public static void main(String[] args) {
        try {
            File file = new File("data.txt");
            Scanner scanner = new Scanner(file);
            while (scanner.hasNextLine()) {
                String line = scanner.nextLine();
                System.out.println(line);
            }
            scanner.close();
        } catch (FileNotFoundException e) {
            System.out.println("Error: File not found.");
        } catch (Exception e) {
            System.out.println("Error: An unexpected error occurred.");
        } finally {
            System.out.println("File reading operation completed.");
        }
    }
}
```

}

In this example, the program attempts to read data from a file named `data.txt`. It handles `FileNotFoundException` if the file is not found and a general `Exception` for any other unexpected errors. The `finally` block ensures that a message is printed regardless of whether an exception is thrown.

By mastering exception handling, students will be able to write more robust and reliable code. Properly handling exceptions ensures that your programs can gracefully recover from errors and continue to function correctly.

CHAPTER 10: FILE HANDLING IN JAVA: READING AND WRITING FILES

File handling is an essential aspect of many applications, allowing you to read from and write to files. This chapter will cover the basics of file handling in Java, including reading files, writing files, and handling file-related exceptions.

Reading Files

To read data from a file, you can use classes such as `File`, `FileReader`, and `BufferedReader`.

Using Scanner

The `Scanner` class can be used to read data from a file:

```java
import java.io.File;
import java.io.FileNotFoundException;
import java.util.Scanner;

public class FileReaderExample {
    public static void main(String[] args) {
        try {
            File file = new File("data.txt");
```

```java
            Scanner scanner = new Scanner(file);
            while (scanner.hasNextLine()) {
                String line = scanner.nextLine();
                System.out.println(line);
            }
            scanner.close();
        } catch (FileNotFoundException e) {
            System.out.println("Error: File not found.");
        }
    }
}
```

Using BufferedReader

The `BufferedReader` class can be used for efficient reading of text files:

java

```java
import java.io.BufferedReader;
import java.io.FileReader;
import java.io.IOException;

public class BufferedReaderExample {
    public static void main(String[] args) {
        try {
            BufferedReader reader = new BufferedReader(new FileReader("data.txt"));
            String line;
            while ((line = reader.readLine()) != null) {
                System.out.println(line);
            }
            reader.close();
        } catch (IOException e) {
            System.out.println("Error: An I/O error occurred.");
        }
    }
}
```

Writing Files

To write data to a file, you can use classes such as FileWriter and BufferedWriter.

Using FileWriter

The FileWriter class can be used to write data to a file:

```java
import java.io.FileWriter;
import java.io.IOException;

public class FileWriterExample {
    public static void main(String[] args) {
        try {
            FileWriter writer = new FileWriter("output.txt");
            writer.write("Hello, World!\n");
            writer.write("This is a test file.");
            writer.close();
            System.out.println("Data has been written to the file.");
        } catch (IOException e) {
            System.out.println("Error: An I/O error occurred.");
        }
    }
}
```

Using BufferedWriter

The BufferedWriter class can be used for efficient writing of text files:

```java
import java.io.BufferedWriter;
import java.io.FileWriter;
import java.io.IOException;

public class BufferedWriterExample {
    public static void main(String[] args) {
        try {
            BufferedWriter writer = new BufferedWriter(new FileWriter("output.txt"));
```

```
            writer.write("Hello, World!\n");
            writer.write("This is a test file.");
            writer.close();
            System.out.println("Data has been written to the file.");
        } catch (IOException e) {
            System.out.println("Error: An I/O error occurred.");
        }
    }
}
```

Handling File-Related Exceptions

File handling operations can throw various exceptions, such as `FileNotFoundException` and `IOException`. It is important to handle these exceptions to ensure your program can gracefully recover from errors.

Example: File Handling with Exception Handling

Let's create a program that reads data from a file and writes data to another file, handling potential exceptions:

java

```java
import java.io.File;
import java.io.FileNotFoundException;
import java.io.FileWriter;
import java.io.IOException;
import java.util.Scanner;

public class FileHandlingExample {
    public static void main(String[] args) {
        try {
            // Reading data from a file
            File inputFile = new File("input.txt");
            Scanner scanner = new Scanner(inputFile);
            StringBuilder data = new StringBuilder();
            while (scanner.hasNextLine()) {
                data.append(scanner.nextLine()).append("\n");
```

```
        }
        scanner.close();

        // Writing data to another file
        FileWriter writer = new FileWriter("output.txt");
        writer.write(data.toString());
        writer.close();
        System.out.println("Data has been read from input.txt and written to output.txt.");
      } catch (FileNotFoundException e) {
        System.out.println("Error: Input file not found.");
      } catch (IOException e) {
        System.out.println("Error: An I/O error occurred.");
      }
   }
}
```

In this example, the program reads data from `input.txt` and writes it to `output.txt`. It handles `FileNotFoundException` if the input file is not found and `IOException` for any other I/O errors.

By mastering file handling, students will be able to create applications that can read from and write to files, enabling them to manage data efficiently. Proper exception handling ensures that your programs can handle file-related errors gracefully and continue to function correctly.

CHAPTER 11: GUI PROGRAMMING: CREATING WINDOWS WITH SWING

Graphical User Interface (GUI) programming allows you to create visually interactive applications. This chapter will cover the basics of GUI programming in Java using the Swing library, including creating windows, adding components, and handling events.

Introduction to Swing

Swing is a part of Java Foundation Classes (JFC) that provides a set of GUI components for building desktop applications. Swing components are lightweight, platform-independent, and flexible.

Setting Up Swing

To use Swing, you need to import the necessary classes from the javax.swing package:

```java
import javax.swing.*;
```

Creating a Simple Window

A basic Swing application consists of a main window (JFrame) and various components such as buttons, labels, and text fields.

java

```java
import javax.swing.*;

public class SimpleWindow {
    public static void main(String[] args) {
        // Create a new JFrame
        JFrame frame = new JFrame("Simple Window");
        frame.setSize(400, 300);
        frame.setDefaultCloseOperation(JFrame.EXIT_ON_CLOSE);

        // Create a label and add it to the frame
        JLabel label = new JLabel("Hello, Swing!");
        frame.add(label);

        // Set the frame's visibility to true
        frame.setVisible(true);
    }
}
```

Adding Components

Swing provides a wide range of components such as buttons, text fields, and panels. You can add these components to your frame and arrange them using layout managers.

Buttons and ActionListeners

To create a button and handle its click event, you can use the `JButton` class and `ActionListener` interface:

java

```java
import javax.swing.*;
import java.awt.event.ActionEvent;
import java.awt.event.ActionListener;

public class ButtonExample {
    public static void main(String[] args) {
```

```java
        JFrame frame = new JFrame("Button Example");
        frame.setSize(400, 300);
        frame.setDefaultCloseOperation(JFrame.EXIT_ON_CLOSE);

        JButton button = new JButton("Click Me");
        button.addActionListener(new ActionListener() {
            public void actionPerformed(ActionEvent e) {
                JOptionPane.showMessageDialog(null, "Button Clicked!");
            }
        });

        frame.add(button);
        frame.setVisible(true);
    }
}
```

Text Fields and Labels

To create text fields and labels, you can use the JTextField and JLabel classes:

java

```java
import javax.swing.*;
import java.awt.event.ActionEvent;
import java.awt.event.ActionListener;

public class TextFieldExample {
    public static void main(String[] args) {
        JFrame frame = new JFrame("Text Field Example");
        frame.setSize(400, 300);
        frame.setDefaultCloseOperation(JFrame.EXIT_ON_CLOSE);
        frame.setLayout(new BoxLayout(frame.getContentPane(), BoxLayout.Y_AXIS));

        JLabel label = new JLabel("Enter your name:");
        JTextField textField = new JTextField(20);
        JButton button = new JButton("Submit");

        button.addActionListener(new ActionListener() {
```

```java
            public void actionPerformed(ActionEvent e) {
                String name = textField.getText();
                JOptionPane.showMessageDialog(null, "Hello, " + name + "!");
            }
        });

        frame.add(label);
        frame.add(textField);
        frame.add(button);
        frame.setVisible(true);
    }
}
```

Layout Managers

Layout managers are used to arrange components within a container. Commonly used layout managers include FlowLayout, BorderLayout, GridLayout, and BoxLayout.

Using FlowLayout

The FlowLayout manager arranges components in a left-to-right flow, similar to text in a paragraph:

java

```java
import javax.swing.*;
import java.awt.*;

public class FlowLayoutExample {
    public static void main(String[] args) {
        JFrame frame = new JFrame("Flow Layout Example");
        frame.setSize(400, 300);
        frame.setDefaultCloseOperation(JFrame.EXIT_ON_CLOSE);
        frame.setLayout(new FlowLayout());

        frame.add(new JButton("Button 1"));
        frame.add(new JButton("Button 2"));
        frame.add(new JButton("Button 3"));
```

```
        frame.setVisible(true);
    }
}
```

Using BorderLayout

The `BorderLayout` manager arranges components in five regions: north, south, east, west, and center:

java

```
import javax.swing.*;
import java.awt.*;

public class BorderLayoutExample {
    public static void main(String[] args) {
        JFrame frame = new JFrame("Border Layout Example");
        frame.setSize(400, 300);
        frame.setDefaultCloseOperation(JFrame.EXIT_ON_CLOSE);
        frame.setLayout(new BorderLayout());

        frame.add(new JButton("North"), BorderLayout.NORTH);
        frame.add(new JButton("South"), BorderLayout.SOUTH);
        frame.add(new JButton("East"), BorderLayout.EAST);
        frame.add(new JButton("West"), BorderLayout.WEST);
        frame.add(new JButton("Center"), BorderLayout.CENTER);

        frame.setVisible(true);
    }
}
```

Using GridLayout

The `GridLayout` manager arranges components in a grid of cells, with each component taking one cell:

java

```
import javax.swing.*;
import java.awt.*;

public class GridLayoutExample {
```

```java
public static void main(String[] args) {
    JFrame frame = new JFrame("Grid Layout Example");
    frame.setSize(400, 300);
    frame.setDefaultCloseOperation(JFrame.EXIT_ON_CLOSE);
    frame.setLayout(new GridLayout(2, 3)); // 2 rows, 3 columns

    frame.add(new JButton("Button 1"));
    frame.add(new JButton("Button 2"));
    frame.add(new JButton("Button 3"));
    frame.add(new JButton("Button 4"));
    frame.add(new JButton("Button 5"));
    frame.add(new JButton("Button 6"));

    frame.setVisible(true);
    }
}
```

Example: Simple Calculator

Let's create a simple calculator with a GUI using Swing:

java

```
import javax.swing.*;
import java.awt.*;
import java.awt.event.ActionEvent;
import java.awt.event.ActionListener;

public class SimpleCalculator {
    public static void main(String[] args) {
        JFrame frame = new JFrame("Simple Calculator");
        frame.setSize(400, 300);
        frame.setDefaultCloseOperation(JFrame.EXIT_ON_CLOSE);
        frame.setLayout(new GridLayout(5, 2));

        JLabel label1 = new JLabel("Number 1:");
        JTextField textField1 = new JTextField();
        JLabel label2 = new JLabel("Number 2:");
        JTextField textField2 = new JTextField();
```

```java
JLabel label3 = new JLabel("Result:");
JTextField resultField = new JTextField();
resultField.setEditable(false);

JButton addButton = new JButton("Add");
JButton subtractButton = new JButton("Subtract");
JButton multiplyButton = new JButton("Multiply");
JButton divideButton = new JButton("Divide");

addButton.addActionListener(new ActionListener() {
    public void actionPerformed(ActionEvent e) {
        try {
            double num1 = Double.parseDouble(textField1.getText());
            double num2 = Double.parseDouble(textField2.getText());
            double result = num1 + num2;
            resultField.setText(String.valueOf(result));
        } catch (NumberFormatException ex) {
            JOptionPane.showMessageDialog(null, "Invalid input.");
        }
    }
});

subtractButton.addActionListener(new ActionListener() {
    public void actionPerformed(ActionEvent e) {
        try {
            double num1 = Double.parseDouble(textField1.getText());
            double num2 = Double.parseDouble(textField2.getText());
            double result = num1 - num2;
            resultField.setText(String.valueOf(result));
        } catch (NumberFormatException ex) {
            JOptionPane.showMessageDialog(null, "Invalid input.");
```

```java
            }
        }
    });

    multiplyButton.addActionListener(new ActionListener() {
        public void actionPerformed(ActionEvent e) {
            try {
                double num1 = Double.parseDouble(textField1.getText());
                double num2 = Double.parseDouble(textField2.getText());
                double result = num1 * num2;
                resultField.setText(String.valueOf(result));
            } catch (NumberFormatException ex) {
                JOptionPane.showMessageDialog(null, "Invalid input.");
            }
        }
    });

    divideButton.addActionListener(new ActionListener() {
        public void actionPerformed(ActionEvent e) {
            try {
                double num1 = Double.parseDouble(textField1.getText());
                double num2 = Double.parseDouble(textField2.getText());
                if (num2 != 0) {
                    double result = num1 / num2;
                    resultField.setText(String.valueOf(result));
                } else {
                    JOptionPane.showMessageDialog(null, "Division by zero is not allowed.");
                }
            } catch (NumberFormatException ex) {
                JOptionPane.showMessageDialog(null, "Invalid
```

```
input.");
            }
        }
    });

    frame.add(label1);
    frame.add(textField1);
    frame.add(label2);
    frame.add(textField2);
    frame.add(label3);
    frame.add(resultField);
    frame.add(addButton);
    frame.add(subtractButton);
    frame.add(multiplyButton);
    frame.add(divideButton);

    frame.setVisible(true);
    }
}
```

In this example, the program creates a simple calculator with buttons for addition, subtraction, multiplication, and division. It uses `GridLayout` to arrange the components and handles button click events to perform calculations.

By mastering GUI programming with Swing, students will be able to create visually interactive applications that enhance the user experience. Understanding the basics of creating windows, adding components, and handling events is essential for developing desktop applications in Java.

CHAPTER 12: APPLETS AND JAVAFX: ADVANCED GUI TECHNIQUES

In addition to Swing, Java provides other frameworks for creating graphical user interfaces, including Applets and JavaFX. This chapter will cover the basics of Applets and JavaFX, demonstrating how to create advanced GUI applications.

Applets

Applets are small Java programs that run within a web browser. They are typically used to create interactive web applications. However, with the decline of support for Applets in modern browsers, their usage has diminished.

Creating an Applet

To create an Applet, extend the `Applet` class and override its methods, such as `init`, `start`, `stop`, and `destroy`:

java

```
import java.applet.Applet;
import java.awt.Graphics;

public class SimpleApplet extends Applet {
```

```java
    public void init() {
        // Initialization code
    }

    public void paint(Graphics g) {
        g.drawString("Hello, Applet!", 50, 50);
    }
}
```

To run the Applet, you need an HTML file with an `<applet>` tag:

html

```html
<!DOCTYPE html>
<html>
<body>
    <applet code="SimpleApplet.class" width="300" height="200"></applet>
</body>
</html>
```

JavaFX

JavaFX is a modern framework for building rich internet applications with a lightweight user interface API. It is designed to replace Swing as the new standard for GUI development in Java.

Setting Up JavaFX

To use JavaFX, you need to include the JavaFX library in your project. You can download it from the official website or use a build tool like Maven or Gradle.

Creating a Simple JavaFX Application

A basic JavaFX application consists of a main class that extends `Application` and overrides the `start` method:

java

```java
import javafx.application.Application;
```

```java
import javafx.scene.Scene;
import javafx.scene.control.Label;
import javafx.stage.Stage;

public class SimpleJavaFXApp extends Application {
    @Override
    public void start(Stage primaryStage) {
        Label label = new Label("Hello, JavaFX!");
        Scene scene = new Scene(label, 400, 300);
        primaryStage.setScene(scene);
        primaryStage.setTitle("Simple JavaFX Application");
        primaryStage.show();
    }

    public static void main(String[] args) {
        launch(args);
    }
}
```

Adding Components

JavaFX provides a wide range of UI controls, such as buttons, text fields, and labels. You can add these components to your scene and arrange them using layout containers.

java

```java
import javafx.application.Application;
import javafx.scene.Scene;
import javafx.scene.control.Button;
import javafx.scene.control.Label;
import javafx.scene.layout.VBox;
import javafx.stage.Stage;

public class ButtonExample extends Application {
    @Override
    public void start(Stage primaryStage) {
        Label label = new Label("Click the button:");
```

```java
        Button button = new Button("Click Me");
        button.setOnAction(e -> label.setText("Button Clicked!"));

        VBox vbox = new VBox(label, button);
        Scene scene = new Scene(vbox, 400, 300);
        primaryStage.setScene(scene);
        primaryStage.setTitle("Button Example");
        primaryStage.show();
    }

    public static void main(String[] args) {
        launch(args);
    }
}
```

Layout Containers

JavaFX provides several layout containers, such as `HBox`, `VBox`, `BorderPane`, `GridPane`, and `StackPane`, to arrange UI components.

Using VBox

The `VBox` layout container arranges its children in a vertical column:

java

```java
import javafx.application.Application;
import javafx.scene.Scene;
import javafx.scene.control.Button;
import javafx.scene.layout.VBox;
import javafx.stage.Stage;

public class VBoxExample extends Application {
    @Override
    public void start(Stage primaryStage) {
        Button button1 = new Button("Button 1");
        Button button2 = new Button("Button 2");
        Button button3 = new Button("Button 3");

        VBox vbox = new VBox(button1, button2, button3);
```

```java
        Scene scene = new Scene(vbox, 400, 300);
        primaryStage.setScene(scene);
        primaryStage.setTitle("VBox Example");
        primaryStage.show();
    }

    public static void main(String[] args) {
        launch(args);
    }
}
```

Using BorderPane

The `BorderPane` layout container arranges its children in five regions: top, bottom, left, right, and center:

java

```java
import javafx.application.Application;
import javafx.scene.Scene;
import javafx.scene.control.Button;
import javafx.scene.layout.BorderPane;
import javafx.stage.Stage;

public class BorderPaneExample extends Application {
    @Override
    public void start(Stage primaryStage) {
        Button topButton = new Button("Top");
        Button bottomButton = new Button("Bottom");
        Button leftButton = new Button("Left");
        Button rightButton = new Button("Right");
        Button centerButton = new Button("Center");

        BorderPane borderPane = new BorderPane();
        borderPane.setTop(topButton);
        borderPane.setBottom(bottomButton);
        borderPane.setLeft(leftButton);
        borderPane.setRight(rightButton);
        borderPane.setCenter(centerButton);
```

```java
        Scene scene = new Scene(borderPane, 400, 300);
        primaryStage.setScene(scene);
        primaryStage.setTitle("BorderPane Example");
        primaryStage.show();
    }

    public static void main(String[] args) {
        launch(args);
    }
}
```

Handling Events

JavaFX uses event handlers to handle user actions. You can set event handlers on UI components to respond to events such as button clicks.

java

```
import javafx.application.Application;
import javafx.scene.Scene;
import javafx.scene.control.Button;
import javafx.scene.layout.VBox;
import javafx.stage.Stage;

public class EventHandlingExample extends Application {
    @Override
    public void start(Stage primaryStage) {
        Button button = new Button("Click Me");
        button.setOnAction(e    ->    System.out.println("Button Clicked!"));

        VBox vbox = new VBox(button);
        Scene scene = new Scene(vbox, 400, 300);
        primaryStage.setScene(scene);
        primaryStage.setTitle("Event Handling Example");
        primaryStage.show();
    }

    public static void main(String[] args) {
```

```
        launch(args);
    }
}
```

Example: Simple JavaFX Calculator

Let's create a simple calculator with a GUI using JavaFX:

java

```
import javafx.application.Application;
import javafx.scene.Scene;
import javafx.scene.control.Button;
import javafx.scene.control.Label;
import javafx.scene.control.TextField;
import javafx.scene.layout.GridPane;
import javafx.stage.Stage;

public class SimpleJavaFXCalculator extends Application {
    @Override
    public void start(Stage primaryStage) {
        Label label1 = new Label("Number 1:");
        TextField textField1 = new TextField();
        Label label2 = new Label("Number 2:");
        TextField textField2 = new TextField();
        Label resultLabel = new Label("Result:");
        TextField resultField = new TextField();
        resultField.setEditable(false);

        Button addButton = new Button("Add");
        Button subtractButton = new Button("Subtract");
        Button multiplyButton = new Button("Multiply");
        Button divideButton = new Button("Divide");

        addButton.setOnAction(e -> {
            try {
                double num1 = Double.parseDouble(textField1.getText());
                double num2 =
```

```java
Double.parseDouble(textField2.getText());
            double result = num1 + num2;
            resultField.setText(String.valueOf(result));
        } catch (NumberFormatException ex) {
            resultField.setText("Invalid input.");
        }
    });

    subtractButton.setOnAction(e -> {
        try {
            double num1 = Double.parseDouble(textField1.getText());
            double num2 = Double.parseDouble(textField2.getText());
            double result = num1 - num2;
            resultField.setText(String.valueOf(result));
        } catch (NumberFormatException ex) {
            resultField.setText("Invalid input.");
        }
    });

    multiplyButton.setOnAction(e -> {
        try {
            double num1 = Double.parseDouble(textField1.getText());
            double num2 = Double.parseDouble(textField2.getText());
            double result = num1 * num2;
            resultField.setText(String.valueOf(result));
        } catch (NumberFormatException ex) {
            resultField.setText("Invalid input.");
        }
    });

    divideButton.setOnAction(e -> {
        try {
            double num1 =
```

```java
                Double.parseDouble(textField1.getText());
                double num2 = Double.parseDouble(textField2.getText());
                if (num2 != 0) {
                    double result = num1 / num2;
                    resultField.setText(String.valueOf(result));
                } else {
                    resultField.setText("Division by zero is not allowed.");
                }
            } catch (NumberFormatException ex) {
                resultField.setText("Invalid input.");
            }
        });

        GridPane gridPane = new GridPane();
        gridPane.add(label1, 0, 0);
        gridPane.add(textField1, 1, 0);
        gridPane.add(label2, 0, 1);
        gridPane.add(textField2, 1, 1);
        gridPane.add(resultLabel, 0, 2);
        gridPane.add(resultField, 1, 2);
        gridPane.add(addButton, 0, 3);
        gridPane.add(subtractButton, 1, 3);
        gridPane.add(multiplyButton, 0, 4);
        gridPane.add(divideButton, 1, 4);

        Scene scene = new Scene(gridPane, 400, 300);
        primaryStage.setScene(scene);
        primaryStage.setTitle("Simple JavaFX Calculator");
        primaryStage.show();
    }

    public static void main(String[] args) {
        launch(args);
    }
}
```

In this example, the program creates a simple calculator with buttons for addition, subtraction, multiplication, and division. It uses `GridPane` to arrange the components and handles button click events to perform calculations.

By mastering advanced GUI techniques with Applets and JavaFX, students will be able to create sophisticated and interactive applications. Understanding the basics of creating applets, JavaFX applications, and handling events is essential for developing rich internet applications in Java.

CHAPTER 13: JAVA LIBRARIES: UTILIZING BUILT-IN FUNCTIONS

Java provides a rich set of built-in libraries that offer a wide range of functionality, from data structures and algorithms to networking and concurrency. This chapter will cover some of the most commonly used Java libraries and demonstrate how to utilize their built-in functions.

Java Standard Library

The Java Standard Library, also known as the Java API, provides a comprehensive set of classes and interfaces for various programming tasks. Some of the key packages include:

- java.lang: Contains fundamental classes such as String, Math, Integer, and System.
- java.util: Provides utility classes such as ArrayList, HashMap, Date, and Collections.
- java.io: Contains classes for input and output operations, such as File, FileReader, FileWriter, and BufferedReader.
- java.net: Provides classes for networking, such as Socket, ServerSocket, URL, and HttpURLConnection.

Using the Math Class

The Math class provides methods for performing basic numeric operations such as exponentiation, logarithms, square roots, and trigonometric functions.

java

```
public class MathExample {
    public static void main(String[] args) {
        double x = 2.0;
        double y = 3.0;

        System.out.println("x = " + x);
        System.out.println("y = " + y);

        System.out.println("Math.pow(x, y) = " + Math.pow(x, y));
        System.out.println("Math.sqrt(x) = " + Math.sqrt(x));
        System.out.println("Math.sin(x) = " + Math.sin(x));
        System.out.println("Math.cos(x) = " + Math.cos(x));
        System.out.println("Math.log(x) = " + Math.log(x));
        System.out.println("Math.exp(x) = " + Math.exp(x));
    }
}
```

Using the Collections Class

The Collections class provides static methods for manipulating collections, such as sorting, searching, and shuffling.

java

```
import java.util.ArrayList;
import java.util.Collections;

public class CollectionsExample {
    public static void main(String[] args) {
        ArrayList<Integer> list = new ArrayList<>();
        list.add(5);
        list.add(2);
```

```
        list.add(9);
        list.add(1);
        list.add(3);

        System.out.println("Original List: " + list);

        Collections.sort(list);
        System.out.println("Sorted List: " + list);

        Collections.shuffle(list);
        System.out.println("Shuffled List: " + list);

        int index = Collections.binarySearch(list, 9);
        System.out.println("Index of 9: " + index);
    }
}
```

Using the Date and Calendar Classes

The `Date` and `Calendar` classes are used for working with dates and times.

java

```
import java.util.Date;
import java.util.Calendar;

public class DateExample {
    public static void main(String[] args) {
        Date now = new Date();
        System.out.println("Current Date and Time: " + now);

        Calendar calendar = Calendar.getInstance();
        calendar.set(2024, Calendar.JUNE, 27);
        Date specificDate = calendar.getTime();
        System.out.println("Specific Date: " + specificDate);

        calendar.add(Calendar.DAY_OF_MONTH, 5);
        Date futureDate = calendar.getTime();
        System.out.println("Future Date: " + futureDate);
    }
```

}

Using the File Class

The File class provides methods for working with files and directories.

java

```
import java.io.File;

public class FileExample {
    public static void main(String[] args) {
        File file = new File("example.txt");

        if (file.exists()) {
            System.out.println("File exists.");
            System.out.println("File name: " + file.getName());
            System.out.println("Absolute path: " + file.getAbsolutePath());
            System.out.println("Writeable: " + file.canWrite());
            System.out.println("Readable: " + file.canRead());
            System.out.println("File size in bytes: " + file.length());
        } else {
            System.out.println("File does not exist.");
        }
    }
}
```

Using the Socket Class

The Socket class provides methods for creating and managing network connections.

java

```
import java.io.IOException;
import java.io.InputStream;
import java.io.OutputStream;
import java.net.Socket;

public class SocketExample {
```

```java
    public static void main(String[] args) {
        try {
            Socket socket = new Socket("example.com", 80);
            OutputStream outputStream = socket.getOutputStream();
            InputStream inputStream = socket.getInputStream();

            String request = "GET / HTTP/1.1\r\nHost: example.com \r\n\r\n";
            outputStream.write(request.getBytes());

            int data;
            while ((data = inputStream.read()) != -1) {
                System.out.print((char) data);
            }

            socket.close();
        } catch (IOException e) {
            e.printStackTrace();
        }
    }
}
```

Example: Using Multiple Libraries

Let's create a program that uses multiple libraries to perform various tasks, such as reading a file, sorting its lines, and printing the sorted lines.

java

```java
import java.io.BufferedReader;
import java.io.FileReader;
import java.io.IOException;
import java.util.ArrayList;
import java.util.Collections;

public class MultiLibraryExample {
    public static void main(String[] args) {
        ArrayList<String> lines = new ArrayList<>();
```

```java
        try (BufferedReader reader = new BufferedReader(new FileReader("data.txt"))) {
            String line;
            while ((line = reader.readLine()) != null) {
                lines.add(line);
            }
        } catch (IOException e) {
            e.printStackTrace();
        }

        Collections.sort(lines);
        for (String line : lines) {
            System.out.println(line);
        }
    }
}
```

In this example, the program reads lines from a file using BufferedReader, stores them in an ArrayList, sorts the lines using Collections.sort, and prints the sorted lines.

By mastering the use of Java libraries, students will be able to leverage built-in functions to simplify complex tasks and enhance their applications. Understanding how to utilize the Java Standard Library effectively is essential for efficient and productive Java programming.

CHAPTER 14: DEBUGGING AND TESTING: ENSURING CODE QUALITY

Debugging and testing are critical aspects of software development that ensure the reliability and correctness of your code. This chapter will cover the basics of debugging and testing in Java, including using debuggers, writing test cases, and using testing frameworks.

Debugging

Debugging is the process of identifying and fixing errors or bugs in your code. Java provides various tools and techniques for effective debugging.

Using Print Statements

One of the simplest debugging techniques is to use print statements (System.out.println) to display the values of variables and the flow of execution.

java

```
public class DebugExample {
    public static void main(String[] args) {
        int a = 5;
```

```
    int b = 0;
    System.out.println("a = " + a);
    System.out.println("b = " + b);

    try {
       int result = a / b;
       System.out.println("Result = " + result);
    } catch (ArithmeticException e) {
       System.out.println("Error: Division by zero.");
    }
  }
}
```

Using a Debugger

Integrated development environments (IDEs) such as Eclipse, IntelliJ IDEA, and NetBeans provide built-in debuggers that allow you to set breakpoints, step through code, and inspect variables.

1. **Setting Breakpoints**: Breakpoints are markers set in the code where the debugger will pause execution, allowing you to inspect the program's state.
2. **Stepping Through Code**: Step through the code line by line to observe the flow of execution and identify where errors occur.
3. **Inspecting Variables**: Inspect the values of variables at different points in the code to understand their state and identify any anomalies.

Testing

Testing is the process of verifying that your code behaves as expected. Java provides various testing frameworks and techniques for effective testing.

Writing Test Cases

A test case is a set of conditions or inputs used to test a

specific aspect of your code. Test cases help ensure that your code produces the expected output for different inputs.

java

```java
public class Calculator {
    public int add(int a, int b) {
        return a + b;
    }

    public int subtract(int a, int b) {
        return a - b;
    }
}

public class CalculatorTest {
    public static void main(String[] args) {
        Calculator calculator = new Calculator();

        // Test case 1: Addition
        int result1 = calculator.add(2, 3);
        if (result1 == 5) {
            System.out.println("Test case 1 passed.");
        } else {
            System.out.println("Test case 1 failed.");
        }

        // Test case 2: Subtraction
        int result2 = calculator.subtract(5, 3);
        if (result2 == 2) {
            System.out.println("Test case 2 passed.");
        } else {
            System.out.println("Test case 2 failed.");
        }
    }
}
```

Using JUnit

JUnit is a popular testing framework for Java that simplifies writing and running test cases. To use JUnit, you need to include the JUnit library in your project.

Writing JUnit Test Cases

JUnit test cases are written in classes that use the @Test annotation to mark test methods. Assertions are used to check the expected outcomes.

java

```
import org.junit.Test;
import static org.junit.Assert.assertEquals;

public class CalculatorTest {
   @Test
   public void testAdd() {
      Calculator calculator = new Calculator();
      int result = calculator.add(2, 3);
      assertEquals(5, result);
   }

   @Test
   public void testSubtract() {
      Calculator calculator = new Calculator();
      int result = calculator.subtract(5, 3);
      assertEquals(2, result);
   }
}
```

Running JUnit Tests

JUnit tests can be run from the command line, an IDE, or build tools like Maven and Gradle. The test results show which test cases passed or failed, along with any errors or failures.

Using TestNG

TestNG is another popular testing framework that offers additional features such as parallel test execution, data-driven testing, and flexible test configurations.

Writing TestNG Test Cases

TestNG test cases are similar to JUnit test cases and use annotations to define test methods, configuration methods, and data providers.

java

```
import org.testng.annotations.Test;
import static org.testng.Assert.assertEquals;

public class CalculatorTest {
   @Test
   public void testAdd() {
      Calculator calculator = new Calculator();
      int result = calculator.add(2, 3);
      assertEquals(result, 5);
   }

   @Test
   public void testSubtract() {
      Calculator calculator = new Calculator();
      int result = calculator.subtract(5, 3);
      assertEquals(result, 2);
   }
}
```

Running TestNG Tests

TestNG tests can be run from the command line, an IDE, or build tools like Maven and Gradle. TestNG provides detailed test reports and logs to help you analyze the test results.

Example: Testing a Banking Application

Let's create a simple banking application and write test cases using JUnit to test its functionality.

java

```java
public class BankAccount {
    private String accountNumber;
    private double balance;

    public BankAccount(String accountNumber, double initialBalance) {
        this.accountNumber = accountNumber;
        this.balance = initialBalance;
    }

    public void deposit(double amount) {
        if (amount > 0) {
            balance += amount;
        }
    }

    public void withdraw(double amount) {
        if (amount > 0 && amount <= balance) {
            balance -= amount;
        }
    }

    public double getBalance() {
        return balance;
    }
}
import org.junit.Test;
import static org.junit.Assert.assertEquals;

public class BankAccountTest {
    @Test
    public void testDeposit() {
        BankAccount account = new BankAccount("123456", 1000.0);
        account.deposit(500.0);
        assertEquals(1500.0, account.getBalance(), 0.01);
    }
```

```
    @Test
    public void testWithdraw() {
        BankAccount account = new BankAccount("123456", 1000.0);
        account.withdraw(200.0);
        assertEquals(800.0, account.getBalance(), 0.01);
    }

    @Test
    public void testWithdrawInsufficientFunds() {
        BankAccount account = new BankAccount("123456", 1000.0);
        account.withdraw(1500.0);
        assertEquals(1000.0, account.getBalance(), 0.01);
    }
}
```

In this example, the `BankAccount` class represents a simple banking application with methods for depositing and withdrawing money. The `BankAccountTest` class contains JUnit test cases to test the functionality of the `BankAccount` class.

By mastering debugging and testing, students will be able to write high-quality, reliable code. Understanding the basics of debugging, writing test cases, and using testing frameworks is essential for ensuring code quality and maintaining software applications.

CHAPTER 15: PROJECT: CREATING A COMPREHENSIVE JAVA APPLICATION

In this final chapter, students will apply the concepts they have learned throughout the book to create a comprehensive Java application. This project will integrate various aspects of Java programming, including object-oriented design, file handling, GUI programming, and testing.

Project Overview

The project is a library management system that allows users to manage a collection of books. The system will support features such as adding new books, searching for books, borrowing and returning books, and displaying the list of books.

Designing the Application

The application will consist of the following classes:

1. Book: Represents a book with properties such as title, author, and availability status.
2. Library: Manages a collection of books and provides methods for adding, searching, borrowing, and

returning books.

3. LibraryGUI: Provides a graphical user interface for interacting with the library.

Book Class

The `Book` class represents a book with properties such as title, author, and availability status.

java

```
public class Book {
    private String title;
    private String author;
    private boolean isAvailable;

    public Book(String title, String author) {
        this.title = title;
        this.author = author;
        this.isAvailable = true;
    }

    public String getTitle() {
        return title;
    }

    public String getAuthor() {
        return author;
    }

    public boolean isAvailable() {
        return isAvailable;
    }

    public void borrow() {
        if (isAvailable) {
            isAvailable = false;
        }
    }

    public void returnBook() {
```

```java
        if (!isAvailable) {
            isAvailable = true;
        }
    }

    @Override
    public String toString() {
        return "Title: " + title + ", Author: " + author + ", Available: " + isAvailable;
    }
}
```

Library Class

The `Library` class manages a collection of books and provides methods for adding, searching, borrowing, and returning books.

java

```java
import java.util.ArrayList;

public class Library {
    private ArrayList<Book> books;

    public Library() {
        books = new ArrayList<>();
    }

    public void addBook(Book book) {
        books.add(book);
    }

    public Book searchBook(String title) {
        for (Book book : books) {
            if (book.getTitle().equalsIgnoreCase(title)) {
                return book;
            }
        }
        return null;
    }
```

```java
    public void borrowBook(String title) {
        Book book = searchBook(title);
        if (book != null && book.isAvailable()) {
            book.borrow();
            System.out.println("Book borrowed: " + book.getTitle());
        } else {
            System.out.println("Book not available.");
        }
    }

    public void returnBook(String title) {
        Book book = searchBook(title);
        if (book != null && !book.isAvailable()) {
            book.returnBook();
            System.out.println("Book returned: " + book.getTitle());
        } else {
            System.out.println("Book not found or already available.");
        }
    }

    public void displayBooks() {
        for (Book book : books) {
            System.out.println(book);
        }
    }
}
```

LibraryGUI Class

The LibraryGUI class provides a graphical user interface for interacting with the library.

java

```
import javafx.application.Application;
import javafx.scene.Scene;
import javafx.scene.control.Button;
import javafx.scene.control.Label;
```

```java
import javafx.scene.control.TextField;
import javafx.scene.layout.GridPane;
import javafx.stage.Stage;

public class LibraryGUI extends Application {
    private Library library;

    @Override
    public void start(Stage primaryStage) {
        library = new Library();

        Label titleLabel = new Label("Title:");
        TextField titleField = new TextField();
        Label authorLabel = new Label("Author:");
        TextField authorField = new TextField();
        Button addButton = new Button("Add Book");
        Button borrowButton = new Button("Borrow Book");
        Button returnButton = new Button("Return Book");
        Button displayButton = new Button("Display Books");

        addButton.setOnAction(e -> {
            String title = titleField.getText();
            String author = authorField.getText();
            if (!title.isEmpty() && !author.isEmpty()) {
                library.addBook(new Book(title, author));
                System.out.println("Book added: " + title);
            }
        });

        borrowButton.setOnAction(e -> {
            String title = titleField.getText();
            if (!title.isEmpty()) {
                library.borrowBook(title);
            }
        });

        returnButton.setOnAction(e -> {
            String title = titleField.getText();
```

```java
            if (!title.isEmpty()) {
                library.returnBook(title);
            }
        });

        displayButton.setOnAction(e -> {
            library.displayBooks();
        });

        GridPane gridPane = new GridPane();
        gridPane.add(titleLabel, 0, 0);
        gridPane.add(titleField, 1, 0);
        gridPane.add(authorLabel, 0, 1);
        gridPane.add(authorField, 1, 1);
        gridPane.add(addButton, 0, 2);
        gridPane.add(borrowButton, 1, 2);
        gridPane.add(returnButton, 0, 3);
        gridPane.add(displayButton, 1, 3);

        Scene scene = new Scene(gridPane, 400, 300);
        primaryStage.setScene(scene);
        primaryStage.setTitle("Library Management System");
        primaryStage.show();
    }

    public static void main(String[] args) {
        launch(args);
    }
}
```

Testing the Application

To ensure the application works correctly, you can write test cases using JUnit to test the functionality of the Library class.

java

```java
import org.junit.Test;
import static org.junit.Assert.assertNotNull;
```

```java
import static org.junit.Assert.assertNull;
import static org.junit.Assert.assertTrue;

public class LibraryTest {
    @Test
    public void testAddAndSearchBook() {
        Library library = new Library();
        Book book = new Book("The Great Gatsby", "F. Scott Fitzgerald");
        library.addBook(book);
        Book foundBook = library.searchBook("The Great Gatsby");
        assertNotNull(foundBook);
    }

    @Test
    public void testBorrowAndReturnBook() {
        Library library = new Library();
        Book book = new Book("1984", "George Orwell");
        library.addBook(book);
        library.borrowBook("1984");
        assertTrue(!book.isAvailable());
        library.returnBook("1984");
        assertTrue(book.isAvailable());
    }
}
```

By completing this project, students will gain hands-on experience in designing, implementing, and testing a comprehensive Java application. This project integrates various aspects of Java programming, providing a practical understanding of how to apply the concepts learned throughout the book.

CONCLUSION

Java Programming for ICSE Students has provided a comprehensive guide to learning Java, covering fundamental concepts, advanced topics, and practical applications. By following the chapters and completing the exercises, students will have gained a solid foundation in Java programming and be well-prepared for their ICSE examinations and future programming endeavors.

www.ingramcontent.com/pod-product-compliance
Lightning Source LLC
Chambersburg PA
CBHW071940210526
45479CB00002B/761